AF477285

Grandmother's memories

This book was filled out by:

____

Time and Place:

____

____

Childhood Memories

Where and when were you born?
Have you ever been told any stories about your birth?

What is your full name? Who named you that and why? Have you ever had a nickname?

What is your earliest childhood memory?

Did you have a favorite toy? Where did you get it?
Do you still have it?

Describe the house you grew up in, and the surroundings.

What is your favorite memory from that house?

What was your favorite food when you were little?
Did you have a favorite dessert, or candy?

Who were your closest friends, growing up?

Did you get an allowance, growing up?
Did you have chores?

Parents
and
Grandparents

Do you know how your parents met?

What did your parents do for a living?

What did they like to do in their spare time?

What Is your favorite memory of your father?

What Is your favorite memory of your mother?

What is the best advice your parents ever gave you?

What were your grandparents like?
What do you remember about them?

Where did your grandparents live?

What did your grandparents do for a living?

Siblings
and
Extended Family

If you have siblings, are they older or younger?
What are your favorite memories of them?

Did you have cousins or other children
that you were close to, growing up?

Are there any features or personality traits that run in your family? Do you have those? Do your children?

What stories have you been told about aunts and uncles
or other family members?

What do you know about your genealogical origins?
Do you have any ancestors from other countries?

School and Adolescence

What was school like for you?
Did you have a favorite subject? A favorite teacher?

When you were in school,
what did you want to be when you grew up? Why?

What did you and your friends do after school as teenagers?
What kind of music did you listen to?

Did you have a curfew as a teenager?
Did you ever miss curfew? Why? What happened?

What did you spend your money on?
Did you ever save up for something special?

Work
and
Adulthood

How old were you when you got your first job? What did you do?

How did you decide on a career?

Did you have a mentor in your chosen career?
A role model? What did that mean to you?

If you could have chosen a different career,
what would that have been and why?

What are some places you have lived?
What was your first own residence?

Did you ever live in another country?
What was that like?

Hobbies
and
Pastimes

What games did you like to play when you were little?

What did you do in your spare time, as a teenager?

Did you ever do any sports? Were you on a team?

Can you play an instrument? Were you ever in a band?

What hobbies have you had? Any collections?

Did you have any pets, growing up?
Have you had any as an adult?

Holidays
and
Celebrations

How did your family celebrate holidays when you were little?

Was your family religious?
Was religion a big part of your childhood?

What is the earliest memory you have of your family at a holiday celebration?

What is your favorite holiday? Why?

Do you have a favorite holiday tradition?

Is there a birthday that stands out in your memory? Why was that day special?

Family Life

When and where did you meet your spouse?

When and where did you get married?
What made you pick that location?

Who was in your wedding? Maid of Honor, Best man,
Groomsmen, Bridesmaids, Ring Bearer, Flower girl?

Did you go on a honeymoon?
What made you pick that particular destination?

How did you pick your children's names?

What are your favorite memories of your children?

Vacations and Adventures

Do you speak any foreign languages?

What was your favorite vacation with your parents?
Why was that vacation so special?

What was your favorite vacation with your own family?

Did you ever travel to another country?
What was that like? Did you bring back any souvenirs?

Do you have a dream destination that you still haven't visited? What made you want to go there?

Have you ever visited a national monument
or a national park?

During
Your
Lifetime

Which world events made an impression on you, growing up?

What is your favorite technological invention that happened during your lifetime?

What is the biggest difference, in your opinion,
between your childhood and your grandchildren's?

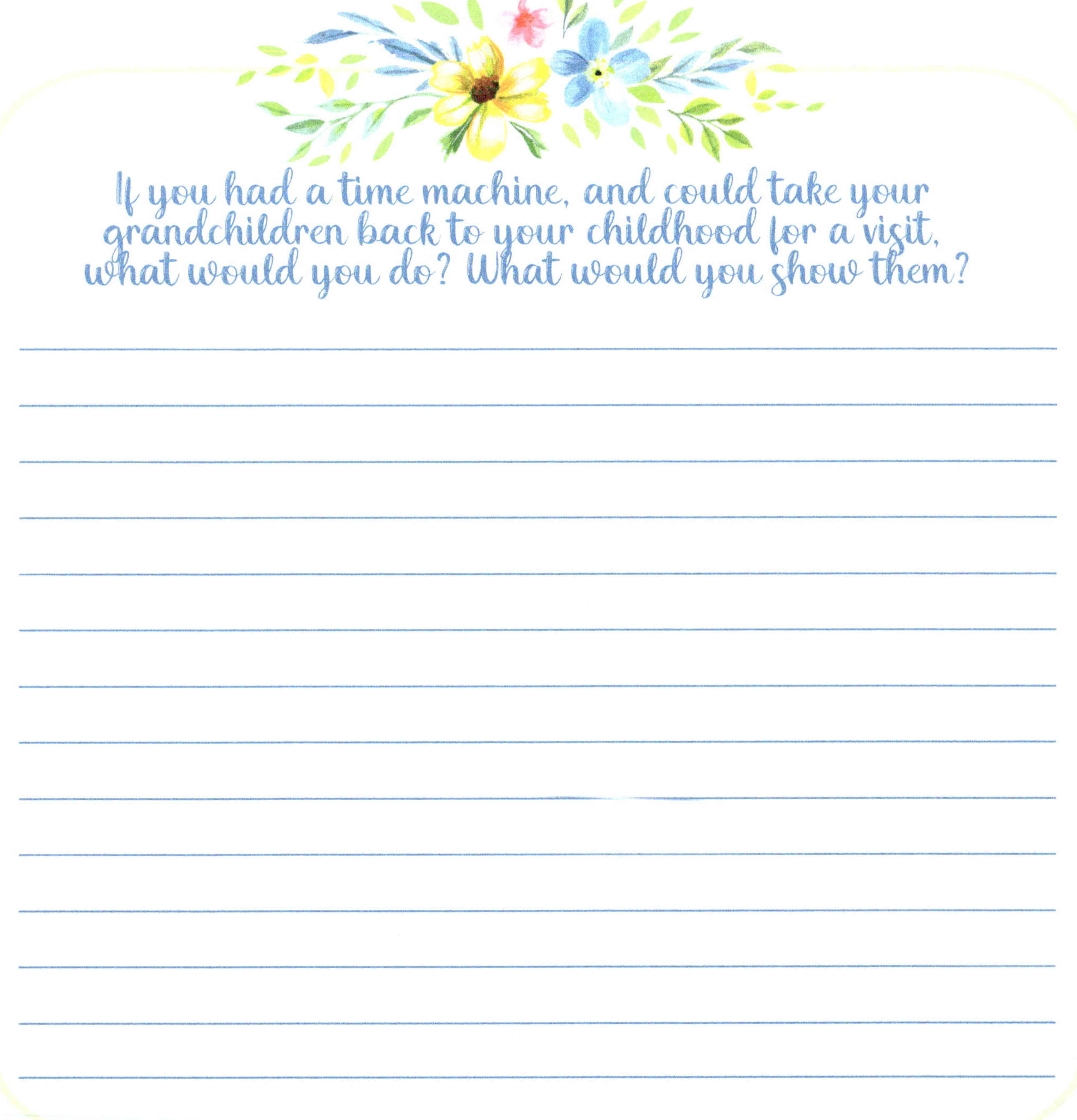

If you had a time machine, and could take your grandchildren back to your childhood for a visit, what would you do? What would you show them?

Getting
to know
Grandma

Do you have a favorite movie? A favorite book? A favorite song?

Have you ever met any celebrities?
Which celebrity would you like to meet?

Are there any family recipes?
Do you have a signature dish?

If you could have lived in a different era,
when would that be? Why?

Is there a special place that means a lot to you?
A place where you've been especially happy?

What accomplishments are you the proudest of?

What would you like your grandchildren to tell their grandchildren about you one day?